# Sweet Dreams

# Sweet Dreams

The Art of
Bessie Pease Gutmann

Written by
Pamela Prince

Illustrated
and
designed
by Christina Donna

Harmony Books/New York

*HARMONY and colophon are trademarks of Crown Publishers, Inc.*
*Manufactured in Japan.*

*Assistant Designer: Mari Yoshimura*

*Library of Congress Cataloging-in-Publication Data*

*Gutmann, Bessie Pease.*
*Sweet dreams.*

*Summary: Illustrations paired with poems show shadow*
*pictures on a rainy day, a dog and a cat coaxed into a*
*momentary truce, and other scenes.*
*1. Gutmann, Bessie Pease. 2. Children's poetry,*
*American—Illustrations. [1. American poetry]*
*I. Prince, Pamela. II. Christina Donna, ill.*
*III. Title.*
*NC975.5.C87A4   1985      741.64'2'0924      84-22400*
*ISBN 0-517-55672-3*

*15   14   13   12*
*First Edition*

*This book is
dedicated with love to
Barbara and Terence
Flynn.*

*D*reamland isn't far away;
It's very near your bed.
It's there beneath the pillow
Where you rest your sleepy head.

How curious, you must agree,
That Dreamland's here each night,
And in the morning when you wake
It vanishes from sight.

Oh, can you think of other lands
That you might recognize,
Ones you can only go to see
When closing shut your eyes?

The time has come to snuggle in
and hug your Teddy Bear.
And off you go together now;
Sweet dreams will take you there.

Some dolls I have are fancier
And some are better dressed.
Some talk, have painted faces
But I think old friends are best.

You've been so true through thick and thin,
You cheer me when I'm glum.
And when I see your trusty smile
I know that you're my chum.

Let others say you're broken
Or you're raggedy and torn;
But you're the one I love to hold
When I wake up each morn.

*Josie was just given a brand new doll in a taffeta dress, but she still loves her raggedy old doll the best.*

*Y*esterday
was warm and fine;
An afternoon most sunny.
Today it's gray and raining out —
So Christopher and Honey
Must play indoors, invent a game
and think of something funny.
Chris throws shadows on the wall
And Oh! oh! There's a bunny!

*Honey
certainly is
surprised to
see a bunny
up on the
wall.*

*C*ats and dogs
don't get along;
At least that's what folks say.
But Josie's pets are friendly
(Almost every other day).
She's always sure to give the dog
A bone that he can bite.
And Mandy gets her bowl of milk
Or else those two might fight
And chase each other 'round the house
As Mandy starts to meow.
Then Jake begins to yap
And drowns out Mandy: BOW-WOW-WOW.
Josie brushed them both today
And scratched behind their ears.
They each got special treats to eat
And so it now appears
They've all they need, they're fed and loved.
Though there's simply no excuse
For them to squabble, this is just
A momentary truce.

*Josie holds
Mandy and Jake,
the friendly
enemies.*

Bessie
Pease
Gutmann

*B*en likes to build things
with his blocks;
A tower or a town.
And just as soon as they're stacked up
His puppy knocks them down.

So patiently the little boy
Begins to build again,
And carefully puts block on block
. . . six, seven, eight, nine, ten.

Temptation's not a thing
That wriggling puppies can ignore;
And once again the wooden blocks
Come tumbling to the floor!

*Benjamin*
*scolds his*
*dog, Danny,*
*for knocking*
*over all the*
*blocks.*

*J*osie's independent.
Now that she has grown
To be three years and seven months
She does things on her own.

She's learning how to make her bed
And proud that she is able
To tie the laces of her shoes
And set the supper table.

This morning Josie brushed her teeth
And combed her curly hair.
As Mama does, she washed her face
Then chose what she would wear.

It only took a second
To don her camisole.
Now. . . just a minute till she slips
The button through its hole.

*Josie's
proud that
she's learned
to do so
many things
on her own;
but she still
has a little
trouble with
buttonholes.*

18

Mama says "Just one more bite
To help you grow up straight and right.
And if you leave an empty dish
You'll get to make a secret wish."
So Tommy spoons his oatmeal up,
Thinking of that furry pup
He saw at the park with Aunt Yvette.
He'd surely like to have a pet,
To cuddle with, to love for good . . .
That's why he gobbles down his food.

*Tommy
eats all his
porridge from
his little
pink bowl,
with hopes
that his wish
will be
granted.*

*T*hat very night his papa brought
A big box home and Tommy thought
That he could guess what was inside
For when the box began to glide
And slide and move from side to side
The little boy let out a shout
And what do you think hopped on out?
A plump and squirming fuzzy pup
Squealed at Tommy and leaped right up!
And from this moment of surprise and joy
They loved each other, dog and boy.

*Tommy's wish
comes true!*

Bessie
Pease
Gutmann

Seven songbirds on a branch
Sing among the trees
Right outside the window
Where a gentle humming breeze
Brings the melody inside
This April afternoon
To little Lizzie's music room.
She imitates the tune.

*Lizzie
listens to
the birds
singing and
likes to
harmonize
with them in
her own
clear, pretty
voice.*

*K*nock, Knock, Knock!
It's one o'clock.
The party starts at two.

We're both all dressed
Up in our best.
Oh, hurry, Mama, do!

*Clara's
best friend,
Cindy, turns
four years
old today.
Clara is so
excited
about going
to the
birthday
party. Her
mama tells
her not to
worry,
they'll get
there in
time.*

$A$nnabelle is patient.
She's instructing Pat the doll.
Patricia never had to learn
(Like Anna) how to crawl.
She leaped directly to her toes
Without a spill or fall,
As long as her kind teacher's there
To guide her down the hall.

*Everything
in life is easier if
you have help
from a good
friend.*

*W*hen you've got a loyal friend,
Someone for whom you care,
Then everything you have
Is what you want to share.

Bessie got an ice cream cone.
She took a tasty lick.
It's only fair, she thought,
That she should offer some to Nick.

*Mama has taught her to be generous, so Bessie thought it would be all right to share her treat with Nick.*

34

$M$ama didn't quite agree
With Bessie's point of view.
For just a little while
The corner's occupied by two.

*Mama
thought
Bessie needed
to be taught
a lesson so
she told her
to stand
in the corner.
She wasn't
really very
angry though
and gave
Bessie a
reprieve
after only five
minutes.*

*H*ere beside a quiet stream
The boy can sit and think and dream;
With his faithful dog as friend
The hours pass without an end.
No one tells him what to do
Or gives him tasks he must pursue.
But he possesses one more wish—
That he could also catch a fish!

*What
a perfectly
peaceful
afternoon
for Jamie
and his
pal.*

*R*ubber balls
are great to bounce;
I like my wooden sled.
Tops are nice to spin and watch;
And my stuffed, fuzzy friend named Ted
Is just about the finest bear
A child could ever own.
But Jake's by far my favorite thing. . .
Why, look at how he's grown!
He's soft and sweet and full of pep;
He plays with me each day
And when I go to bed at night
He'll curl up, sleep, and stay.
I think that he's my dearest friend,
Much better than a toy,
For he's alive and warm and fun,
Just like a little boy.

*Peter thinks his dog, Jake, is better than any toy could ever be.*

*S*oftly singing lullabies,
One by one they close their eyes.
Dolly played so hard today. . .
Off to Dreamland, on her way.
Gentle Jeremy the pup
Curls his furry body up.
Clara, little golden-head,
Soon will make her way to bed.

*Clara,
Jeremy, and
Dolly bring
the day to a
peaceful
close as the
little girl
sings a
good-night
song.*

$U$p you go," his papa said;
So Peter treks his way toward bed.
Legs quite short and tiny feet
Make it hard for Jake and Pete
To reach the top, but still they climb
Step by step, one at a time.
Petey's winning, in the lead
But every night Jake picks up speed
As they near the landing, when
He bursts ahead and barks and then
He races Peter down the hall.
That's when they hear Mama call
"All right, you two, now go to sleep.
Quiet, not another peep."
When she comes in to say "Good night,"
To tuck them in, turn off the light,
They've already closed their eyes.
They're in the Land of Lullabies.

*Peter and
Jake head
upstairs to bed
as Papa says
"Nitey-nite."*

# Night-
night
and
sweet
dreams.